Daily PRAYER BOOK *for BOYS*

Collection of Prayers for Boys to Inspire Courage and Bravery with God

FaithLabs

THIS BOOK BELONGS TO:

. . . .

. . . .

. . . .

. . . .

Daily

PRAYER

BOOK

for BOYS

Collection of Prayers for Boys to Inspire Courage and Bravery with God

Don't Forget Your Free Bonus Downloads!

As our way of saying thank you, we've included in every purchase bonus gift downloads. If you've enjoyed reading this book, please consider leaving a review.

Or Scan Your Phone to open QR code

Daily Prayer Book for Boys:
Collection of Prayers for Boys to Inspire Courage
and Bravery with God

Copyright © 2023

Daily Prayer Book for Boys

Contents

Introduction. 9

Prayers for
Everyday. 13

Prayers for
Needy Times. 31

Prayers for
Praise and Thanks to God. 49

Prayers for
Family and Friends. 67

Prayers for
Love. 85

Prayers for
Spiritual Growth 103

Encouragement to Continue Praying. 121

Quiz Questions. 126

About Us. 131

Daily Prayer Book for Boys

INTRODUCTION

"And this is the confidence that we have in him, that, if we ask anything according to his will, he heareth us." -
1 John 5:14

Things are changed through prayer. Those who have faith in God and experience the efficacy of prayer may attest to this. Yet, what really is prayer, and how should we pray?

To start, the act of praying is holy. If you're meditating to pray, relax and let your thoughts drift. Communicating with God through prayer must be done with absolute sincerity. Avoid the temptation to show off by praying in private. Your prayers will be answered if you are sincere and faithful. We are trained to provide specific requests as part of learning how to pray. Do not be shy about coming to God in prayer with specific requests. Jesus is the only way to get everything we need and seek from God.

Sincerity, modesty, and an absence of hypocrisy are all essential components of effective prayer. Use succinct, to-the-point language as well. If you pray for a long period or use meaningless phrases, your request will not be heard any more favorably. You don't have to be a great speaker to have an impact on God; He just wants to hear from your heart. God desires us to enjoy a rich and satisfying existence, but this can only happen if we establish a personal connection with him. Having a conversation with God is something that can be taught, but it requires time, effort, and dedication.

There is no doubt that prayer significantly impacts one's maturation. If you shut your eyes and pray earnestly to God, anything you ask for will come true so long as you don't ask for the destruction of others. You will undoubtedly succeed if you constantly pray daily to God that he will bless you with glory, honor, and prosperity. But you need to realize that God desires you to train your patience. Nothing will happen quickly enough to satisfy your impatience. Only by being patient can you see God's rewards for your efforts.

If you believe in God and pray, you will see miraculous results. It is imperative that we put our whole trust in God. God has unlimited strength and vitality. He takes the shape of comforting light rather than scorching flames. We, like the stars, are the essence of being human. We each have a certain purpose for being here on Earth. Our job is to use the body God has given us to act out our parts on the enormous global stage. To earn God's favor, we need to keep his name in mind and do acts of kindness. This is the only way to find true contentment and lasting success in this life and the next.

Throughout the following chapters, you'll find a variety of prayers suitable for a wide range of situations. Praying regularly may strengthen our connection with God and our prayer life.

Daily Prayer Book for Boys

PART 1

Prayers for Everyday

Morning Prayer And Meditation Of Thanks

*

For God so loved the world, that he gave his only begotten Son, that whosoever believeth in him should not perish, but have everlasting life.

John 3:16

Prayer

Please accept our sincere thanks and praise, Almighty Lord. We sincerely thank you for the gift of sight and hearing this morning. We thank You that You are a God of mercy and compassion. So much has been done for us, and You continue to bless us. Our greatest gratitude is for Jesus Christ, our Lord and Savior. With Jesus' death, burial, and resurrection, we have been forgiven of our sins and brought into Your kingdom for eternity. Amen.

*

Reflection

Every day, we should never forget to thank God for his favors. What blessings are you thankful for today? What recent unexpected blessing have you received?

Prayer For A Blessed Attitude And Gratitude

✳

For I the Lord thy God will hold thy right hand, saying

unto thee, fear not; I will help thee.

Isaiah 41:13

Prayer

Gratitude fills my heart, My Lord, as I praise You for this wonderful morning. I want to approach today with a fresh perspective and an abundance of thankfulness. Instruct me in the path of good living. Thank You, Lord Jesus Christ, for paying the price for my severe sins and suffering. As a sinner needing Your mercy and forgiveness, I praise You for Your sacrifice on the cross. Please accept my gratitude for reconciling us to God the Father and bathing us in unending grace and the promise of redemption. Amen.

Reflection

Optimism that things will work out is an excellent way to start the day. What do you wish for every morning when you get up? What is your perspective on approaching your day?

Starting The Day With Forgiveness

Be careful for nothing; but in every thing by prayer and supplication with thanksgiving let your requests be made known unto God.

Philippians 4:6

Prayer

Lord, today we ask You to pardon us for all the times we have disobeyed You in what we have said, done, or thought. Please protect us from any harm that may come our way. We hope this day will bring a change in perspective and an abundance of thankfulness. Let us use each day to get our thoughts in order and hear from You. Let's not pout and cry about things we can't change. Let us continue to see sin as God does and recognize it for the bad it is. Let us turn from our sins, confessing them aloud so that God may pardon us. Lord, help us hold our tongues and not judge others. Amen.

Reflection

When we mess up, God never holds a grudge against us; rather, he always forgives us. Do you harbor grudges toward those who have wronged you? How can you say you have already forgiven the person who hurt you?

19

Praying For Daily Blessings

And when he had sent the multitudes away, he went up into a mountain apart to pray: and when the evening was come, he was there alone.

Matthew 14:23

Prayer

Lord, please continue to bless us so that we might be a blessing to others around us. Let us remain courageous to aid the outcasts and the vulnerable. Please keep us upbeat so that we may provide words of encouragement to those who need them. God bless the wayward and the confused. Assist those who have been unfairly labeled. Raise those who have been beaten down back to health. Please make us a beacon of hope amid their despair. In the name of God, Jesus Christ, amen.

✳

Reflection

Sharing the love of God with others is what it means to be a blessing to others. How do you introduce people to God? How do you use the gifts God has given you to help others?

Prayer For Peace at Home

And into whatsoever house ye enter, first say, peace be to this house. And if the son of peace be there, your peace shall rest upon it: if not, it shall turn to you again.

Luke 10:5-6

Prayer

We believe in your ability to transform hearts and lives. Lord, may their houses be places of rest, love, and pleasure. Help them pay off their debts and meet all of their basic necessities. Help those who are suffering emotionally and physically. We ask that everyone who hears these words and whose lips voluntarily confess them find acceptance in their hearts. We thank the Lord because He promised to stay with us until the end. We pray for Your coming, Lord Jesus Christ, and look forward to the day Your grace might save us. Amen.

Reflection

We cannot avoid family issues, but family prayer may help us overcome them. What issues does your family now face? How do you address issues inside the family?

Prayer For Strength For The Week Ahead

✳

*With my soul have I desired thee in the night; yea, with
my spirit within me will I seek thee early: for when thy
judgments are in the earth, the inhabitants of the world will
learn righteousness.*

Isaiah 26:9

Prayer

Thanks be to God, I woke up to another beautiful day. Help me get over today's difficulties by walking with me. Infuse me with the courage to face the challenges of this week. My trust in you and reliance on your might will sustain me throughout my day. Please keep me safe this week with the help of Your angels while I follow Your perfect will. May all the things I touch will be blessed. I ask this in the name of Jesus Christ, the Almighty. Amen.

✳

Reflection

Since only God can give us the strength to confront whatever is ahead, we should constantly seek God's direction in everything we do. What's your weekly schedule? What is your regular praying schedule?

Prayer To Overcome Temptations

There hath no temptation taken you but such as is common to man: but God is faithful, who will not suffer you to be tempted above that ye are able; but will with the temptation also make a way to escape, that ye may be able to bear it.

1 Corinthians 10:13

Prayer

Holy God, I ask that You fortify me to resist the world's temptations and stand firm for You. You know that today will not be without challenges for me. I ask for Your comfort and guidance as I face them. Nothing will be out of reach as long as you are at my side. If I am too weak to walk, please carry me. Do anything to turn me into a victor. Give me all the knowledge you have. I ask this in the name of Jesus, the Lord of hosts. Amen.

✳

Reflection

There are temptations everywhere, and it is up to us whether or not we succumb. How do you maintain your concentration on the most essential tasks? What often interferes with your prayer time?

Prayer For Confidence

❋

Thou sendest forth thy spirit, they are created: and thou renewest the face of the earth.

Psalms 104:30

 # Prayer

Lord, I tend to focus on my shortcomings and mistakes too much. When I think of myself in light of this, I feel terrible. Please assist me in completely appreciating the fact that I am uniquely and beautifully formed in your image today. Put a stop to any and all criticism that has been leveled at me. Lord, I need your help to pick up the pieces and get back on my feet. Lord, you have promised that those with self-respect also maintain *umility. Thanks be to God. Amen.

 # Reflection

Our errors do not define us but inspire us to improve ourselves. What do you do when you make a mistake? How can you make amends for this mistake?

Daily Prayer Book for Boys

PART 2

Prayers for Needy Times

Dry My Tears

*

I cried unto the Lord in my distress, and he heard me

Psalms 120:1

Prayer

My Lord, my God, I pray to you, my Sovereign Savior, my Gentle Jesus. Please wipe my tears. Please heal the wounds and soothe the suffering; I give everything to You. When the light comes up, these tears shimmer with a longing for the indescribable happiness they once experienced. Lord God, please catch my tears. Please accept me into Your everlasting arms of love since I am unworthy of anything else. We put our faith in you, Lord, to restore our faithlessness. Raise me up, above and beyond where I've been. Amen.

✳

Reflection

When wounded, pouring our hearts into God is acceptable. When did you last shed a tear? Why were you crying at the time?

My Strength and Joy

I cried unto thee; save me, and I shall keep thy testimonies.

Psalm 119:146

Prayer

Help me, Lord, because I can't do this alone. Fill my heart with happiness even when sorrow threatens. Help me find my way when I get lost, and soothe me when I'm sad. Oh God, please wipe away my tears. I have to get rid of this pain in my chest. Without You, I have no hope. Please, Holy Spirit, come close. Here I am, on my knees. More than ever, I need your assistance. I can always rely on You, Lord, since You have never let me down. Amen.

✳

Reflection

God is the source of our strength and joy. What gives you strength? What does happiness entail for you?

Make me Whole and Brand New

*

They that sow in tears shall reap in joy.

Psalm 126:5

Prayer

No matter how high the winds blow or how strong the waves get, I know I can always find safety in Your wings, Lord. Dancing in the rain is a joy when I wait for You, Lord. Joy, love, peace, and happiness shall enter my life and the lives of those I love from this day on. In the name of Jesus Christ, the Mighty, I ask that You hear my humble supplication and shower me with Your plentiful blessings. Amen.

✽

Reflection

God will only assist us in changing and becoming new if we are willing to change and become new. Which undesirable behaviors do you want to change? What measures are you taking to alter these undesirable behaviors?

Crying Out To God

*

And Asa cried unto the Lord his God, and said, Lord, it is nothing with thee to help, whether with many, or with them that have no power: help us O Lord our God; for we rest on thee, and in thy name we go against this multitude. O Lord, thou art our God; let not man prevail against thee.

2 Chronicles 14:11

Prayer

Jesus Christ, the One and Only God, Whose Reign will never end. All the praise and adoration I have are for Your name, which is worthy of all praise and adoration. I give You thanks and submit to Your control over my life. Oh, Father, You're the best! But now my heart is crushed, and I must weep. Please enlighten me about your mission for me here on earth and the calling You have bestowed upon me. Help me figure out why I'm here and what my life is all about. Amen.

*

Reflection

Each of us has a unique purpose on the planet. How do you share the words of God with your friends? How do you serve God in your household?

Whatever I Ask For

In my distress I called upon the Lord, and cried unto my God: he heard my voice out of his temple, and my cry came before him, even into his ears.

Psalm 18:6

Prayer

Please, Lord God, open my eyes to see that I am completely in Your hands. I believe in Your divine might; therefore, please make it so that my prayers are answered according to Your nature. And Lord, let me hear the quiet, little voice inside, ministering to me at every turn, especially when it is hardest for me to forgive those who have mistreated me. Teach me how to keep my mouth shut when I shouldn't speak out. Amen.

✳

Reflection

God is always in charge of our life. What considerations do you take into account while making a choice? What do you do with the aspects of your life that you cannot control?

My Heart Hurts

*

And he said unto me, my grace is sufficient for thee: for my strength is made perfect in weakness. Most gladly therefore will I rather glory in my infirmities, that the power of Christ may rest upon me. Therefore I take pleasure in infirmities, in reproaches, in necessities, in persecutions, in distresses for Christ's sake: for when I am weak, then am I strong.

2 Corinthians 12:9-10

Prayer

God, who makes me feel worthy of hope and love despite my many flaws, thank you for being there. Although I grumble when others leave my side, you are the only one who has never left mine. It breaks my heart to consider how you must feel. "Be quiet, and know that I am God" I hear you. I will never longer put other people's needs before yours, God. Please don't let go of my heart. Please don't allow anybody including myself to destroy any remaining hope for it. Please keep it safe in your hands until we are both ready to offer it to someone. Amen.

✳

Reflection

God will always love us regardless of our transgressions, and he will never weary of consoling us when we are broken. Do you believe God loves you? How does God demonstrate his love for you?

Above The Hurt And Pain

For I know the thoughts that I think toward you, saith the Lord, thoughts of peace, and not of evil, to give you an expected end.

Jeremiah 29:11

Prayer

Lord, You've given me much more good fortune than I deserved. You must help me prioritize my affection for you. We must put love above everything else wrath, pride, fury, attention, love, doubt, money, people, jobs, schools, churches, everything. If it weren't for your unwavering support, I wouldn't be where I am now. Remind me of this, please. You really care about me and adore me. This stands out to me more than anything else right now. I want to love others as selflessly as you love us. Amen.

Reflection

God tells us to love our neighbors as much as we love ourselves. How do you express your affection for your neighbors? Why is love so essential?

Prayer For When You Feel Broken

*

He healeth the broken in heart, and bindeth up their
wounds. He telleth the number of the stars; he calleth them
all by their names. Great is our Lord, and of great power:
his understanding is infinite.

Psalms 147:3-5

 # Prayer

The pain of a shattered spirit is real, and in the name of Jesus Christ, I beg you to heal it. To the extent that it is possible, I hope today is a tremendous accomplishment for everyone. Don't let anything get in the way of us prioritizing our own happiness. Give us the grace to appreciate everything You've done for us and to find fulfillment in Jesus alone rather than in the company of other people or the possessions You've blessed us with. We hope that You will heal us and bless our endeavors. We won't let obstacles get in our way. Instead, we will learn from Your Word, heed Your guidance, and do what we are told. Amen.

＊

 # Reflection

God is the only healer we need when hurt or wounded. What is the most painful event you have had? How can one repair a broken heart?

Daily Prayer Book for Boys

PART 3

Prayers for Praise and Thanks to God

Thanksgiving Prayer

Rejoice evermore. Pray without ceasing. In every thing give thanks: for this is the will of God in Christ Jesus concerning you.

1 Thessalonians 5:16-18

Prayer

Lord in heaven, we come before you today not to beg for anything but to humbly express our gratitude for all you have done for us. We are grateful to You, Lord, for sending Jesus to suffer for our sins on that old, hard cross. Thank you for bearing so much anguish and pain for our redemption. We ask for the same strength to endure life for the sake of Your glory. Thank you for granting our family health and vitality. Oh Lord, thank you for your daily gift of unconditional, eternal, unfailing, and boundless love. Amen.

Reflection

Jesus gave his life for our salvation. What sacrifices are you willing to make for Christ? What are you ready to do to repay him for his sacrifice?

Giving Thanks for This Day

*

Thanks to God for his unspeakable gift.

2 Corinthians 9:15

Prayer

We praise You, Lord, for awakening us to this beautiful day. We appreciate Your watchful care for our loved ones and us. We offer gratitude for life and all the blessings it has bestowed upon us good health, robust vigor, God's unending love and forgiveness, tranquility, and unwavering joy. Our Lord and Savior, Jesus Christ, is the focus of everything we do, so please direct our steps. Amen.

✳

Reflection

Every new day is a divine gift. What daily prayers do you offer to God? What do you do when your day is going poorly?

Thanks for Blessings

*

O give thanks unto the Lord; for he is good; for his mercy endureth forever.

1 Chronicles 16:34

Prayer

Our gratitude extends to You, Lord, for the ways in which each of life's gifts and challenges have helped us mature into the people we were always intended to be and the ones You've always desired us to be. Each day brings fresh grace and blessings; I am eternally grateful. We praise and thank You for our precious loved ones, the food we eat, and the shelter over our heads. Lord, we thank You that You see our tears, hear our prayers, and know our hearts. We praise and thank the Messiah for everything He has done and will accomplish. I pray this in the name of the Lord Jesus Christ, amen.

✳

Reflection

Never forget to thank God for his daily blessings. Who provides for your family? How do you express gratitude to your parents for all their generosity?

Being Thankful For Your Testimony

*

Giving thanks always for all things unto God and the
Father in the name of our Lord Jesus Christ.

Ephesians 5:20

Prayer

For making me into this, I am eternally grateful. Lord, shape me into the person You want and desire me to be. Knowing You as well as I do has been a tremendous blessing. God, I am humbled and grateful that You have chosen me to serve as a leader, to speak about Your kindness, and to tell how Your grace has changed my life and the lives of others. Amen.

✱

Reflection

All of us are living examples of God's love. Do you frequently serve in the church? What should a servant leader in the church be?

Prayer For The Lord's Will In Your Life

*

Continue in prayer, and watch in the same with thanksgiving.

Colossians 4:2

Prayer

Lord, You are the only one I want. You have my undying love. All glory to You. And now, I give all the credit and honor back to You, our eternal Father. I adore you more than words can say or show. I will always be by Your side. I just want to complete this race. Please tell me You're pleased with me. And I want more than anything to share that happiness with You eventually. Your son relies on you. And in the name of Jesus Christ, I ask all of this. Amen.

*

Reflection

God has plans for our lives. What do you want to accomplish in the future? How do you know whether your actions are God's will?

Thank You, Father, for Answered Prayers

✳

And in that day shall ye say, praise the Lord, call upon his name, declare his doings among the people, make mention that his name is exalted. Sing unto the Lord; for he hath done excellent things: this is known in all the earth.

Isaiah 12:4-5

Prayer

Lord, I offer You the honor and adoration that is Yours. You've been so reliable. Thank the Lord for hearing my prayers and giving me everything I've asked for today. Peace be with me always, and may God's name be praised in the heavens and on earth. Amen.

Reflection

Always persist in our prayers and requests to God for what we want. Have you ever had a prayer go unanswered? What was the outcome of this prayer that went unanswered?

Giving Praise for His Son

By him therefore let us offer the sacrifice of praise to God continually, that is, the fruit of our lips giving thanks to his name.

Hebrews 13:15

Prayer

Merciful Father, I honor You for being the unstoppable force that You are. I worship You on Your throne of grace with all my being. Thank you for giving up your only Son as a sacrifice on my behalf. Christ has given me a new life. His blood was spilled to have a full and prosperous life. So be it; I pray in Jesus' name. Amen.

✳

Reflection

Jesus entered the world in order to rescue us. What would you say about Jesus? What role does Jesus have in your life?

Prayer of Gratitude for a Renewed Mind

*

Cease not to give thanks for you, making mention of you in my prayers.

Ephesians 1:16

Prayer

I give You praise and thanks because You have made me into the person You want me to be by renewing my mind in Your holy Word. You have made me more than a conqueror; you have given me the power to overcome life's challenges. Through faith, I acknowledge that in Christ Jesus, I have been made righteous before God. I appreciate being created in God's likeness, so thank you for that. I'm not like anybody else; I'm a one-of-a-kind creation shaped by the tender yearnings of Your soul. Amen.

❋

Reflection

We were formed in the image and likeness of God. What do you take this remark to mean? How are we similar to God?

Daily Prayer Book for Boys

PART 4

Prayers for Family and Friends

Wisdom And Understanding In My Family

*

And let the peace of God rule in your hearts, to the which

also ye are called in one body; and be ye thankful.

Colossians 3:15

Prayer

Lord, I ask for your guidance as we face the difficulties and make the choices that life presents. We prioritize you and your will above all else in everything we do. I ask that you keep our loved ones safe and sound and strengthen our bonds as a family in our shared faith. Our love for one another should mirror your love for us, and may it shine brightly before others. Amen.

Reflection

Problems facing the family should be addressed together. What difficulties have you encountered in your family? How did you overcome these obstacles?

Prayer For My Parents

Honour thy father and thy mother: that thy days may be long upon the land which the Lord thy God giveth thee.

Exodus 20:12

Prayer

With a grateful heart, I pray to you, Lord, on behalf of my parents. I ask that you bless and watch after them because of all the love and support they have given me. I pray that they will have a complete revelation of God's love. I ask that you bless them with fortitude and bravery to overcome any difficulties they encounter, and that you provide all of their material necessities. I pray that you'll always be at the center of their attention and that their love for one another never wanes. I ask for these things in the name of Jesus Christ, my Lord and Savior. Amen.

*

Reflection

Our parents will try to provide for us and enrich our lives. What would you say about your parents? How do you honor their sacrifices on your behalf?

Prayer For Better Relationships

✳

Train up a child in the way he should go and when he is old, he will not depart from it.

Proverbs 22:6

Prayer

Father in Heaven, It's baffling that you can be all three things simultaneously. But Lord, we know this: You made the Father, the Son, and the Holy Spirit, and You put them together to make us so that we may love You and be loved by You. Lord, even so, in the realms of earth, you have allowed us to experience the joys of human connection: marriage, parenthood, friendship, and all the rest. We thank You for the many methods by which we are able to interact with others and show them our appreciation, love, and friendship. Amen.

*

Reflection

Our relationships with others are a blessing that we must always cherish. Who is your ideal friend? Why is it essential to have friends in our lives?

Better Relationships between Parents and Children

*

Husbands, love your wives, even as Christ also loved the church, and gave himself for it.

Ephesians 5:25

Prayer

Lord, we thank you for the gift of parental ties, which allow us to know what it's like to rely on another person for everything until we're old enough to do it ourselves. The bond between parents and their children provides a beautiful view into God's heart. We give thanks for the bonds between parents and their offspring. I pray that the members of this family be blessed with an abundance of happiness and tranquility. Amen.

Reflection

Our parents instilled the virtues we will bear into old age. What is one piece of advice that your parents always give you about life? Who offers you the most life advice?

Better Relationships between Friends and Loved Ones

*

Let not mercy and truth forsake thee: bind them about thy neck; write them upon the table of thine heart. So shall thou find favor and good understanding in the sight of God and man.

Proverbs 3:3-4

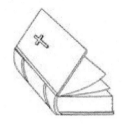

Prayer

We give thanks to you, Lord, for the blessing of good friends and family. Thank you, Lord, for those who listen when we need them and give us advice when we face adversity. Thank you, Father, for all the times you've comforted us with wise counsel, hugged us tight when needed, and listened while we poured our hearts out to you. Lord, I give you thanks for the ways in which the fellowship you enjoy in the Trinity may be seen in the connections amongst your people. Amen.

Reflection

One of God's commands is to develop positive relationships with others. Why is it essential to be kind to others? What influence does kindness have on your life?

Family Declaration

Peace I leave with you, my peace I give unto you: not as the world giveth, give I unto you. Let not your heart be troubled, neither let it be afraid.

John 14.27

Prayer

To the shattered families, we proclaim a just reconstruction. Those that were formerly abandoned are being restored. The Lord is renewing the hearts of the shattered. Those who have been taken advantage of and exploited by family members are declared healed and whole in the name of Jesus. We bind the devil, his forces, and all the forces and principalities of darkness in the Name of Jesus. Those trapped in a cycle of abuse and domestic violence will be free. Our homes are abodes of God's perfect serenity. Amen.

Reflection

Every family is distinct, and we should always pray for those experiencing hardship. Do you know a family that is currently struggling? What steps can you take to help them?

Peace In The Family

*

And let the peace of God rule in your hearts, to the which also ye are called in one body; and be ye thankful.

Colossians 3:15

Prayer

Father in Heaven, I pray for harmony in my household by bringing it before You. Lord my God, my loved ones and I are in a fierce battle with the devil. Heavenly Lord, please grant them courage and put their hearts at rest. Inspire a desire for God's righteousness in their hearts, and they'll be satisfied. Provide for them materially and keep them safe under Your protection. Keep them safe from harm. Wrap them in the purity of Your blood and make them as clean as snow. Amen.

Reflection

A harmonious family relationship is essential to ensure peace at home. What do you do when you have a disagreement with a relative? How do you settle your disputes?

Cry For Salvation Of Family Members

*

- So shall my word be that goeth forth out of my mouth: it shall not return unto me void, but it shall accomplish that which I please, and it shall prosper in the thing whereto I sent it.

Isaiah 55:11

 # Prayer

Every day, Lord, your people pray for the salvation of their loved ones. Oh, God, please bless their families, from the mothers and fathers to the spouses and children. Reduce their physical discomfort. Put an end to all the ill words spoken about them. Wash them in the lamb's blood until they are as pure as snow. They need to be reborn and rescued by your powerful name. Amen.

 # Reflection

Families should support one another in times of hardship. Has your family experienced the prejudice of others? What did you do during this time?

Daily Prayer Book for Boys

PART 5

Prayers for Love

Prayer for Blessings and Love

For, brethren, ye have been called unto liberty; only use not liberty for an occasion to the flesh, but by love serve one another.

Galatians 5:13

Prayer

God the Eternal, every morning, I'm grateful for the gift of air that brings me health, vigor, wealth, and God's favor. Please, Lord, keep blessing me. Help me stay united with Your mercy and kindness. Holy Spirit, if it pleases You, renew and refresh me with the splendor of Your presence. If given the opportunity, I will share Your love with everyone I meet. When Your splendor is seen in me, please bestow upon me the strength of the heavenly realms. Please pour forth Your love through me and show me how I might help others. Amen.

Reflection

Even if we don't ask for it, God provides for our daily needs. What are your daily necessities? Do you believe you have sufficient provisions, and if so, why?

Filled with God's Love

For God so loved the world, that he gave his only begotten Son, that whosoever believeth in him should not perish, but have everlasting life.

John 3:16

Prayer

Lord, fill me with your tranquility, compassion, and love so that I may be a source of goodness to everyone around me. Please help me to be charitable even when I don't feel like it. Show me how to have mercy on people even if I don't believe they deserve it. Please help me show other people the same love you offer me daily. I pray to God that I may be able to forgive those who have hurt me. Those who have never experienced your love have never really known love. I pray that they'll find their way back to you. Amen.

✳

Reflection

God's affection is unconditional, and he still loves us even if we disappoint him. Do you think of yourself as generous? What impact does generosity have on those around us?

Prayer for the Broken and Depressed

*

But God commendeth his love toward us, in that, while we were yet sinners, Christ died for us.

Romans 5:8

Prayer

Please, Lord, be the one who comforts those who are suffering from pain, loneliness, depression, broken hearts, and poor self-esteem and cries out to you. Give them a hug from your soft heart. Open your arms and let them in. Please accompany them on their journey. Help them along and demonstrate your affection. Assist them in remembering that you have promised never to abandon or forsake your followers. God, please give them courage; in the name of Jesus Christ, cure, touch, and rescue them. Amen.

Reflection

Only God's compassion can heal us from all the suffering we are currently experiencing. Have you ever been harmed by others? What did you do to heal from this pain?

Prayer to Show God's Love

*

Bless the Lord, O my soul: and all that is within me, bless his holy name. Bless the Lord, O my soul, and forget not all his benefits: Who forgiveth all thine iniquities; who healeth all thy diseases; Who redeemeth thy life from destruction; who crowneth thee with loving kindness and tender mercies; Who satisfieth thy mouth with good things; so that thy youth is renewed like the eagle's.

Psalm 103:1-5

Prayer

Father, make Your Word our daily nourishment, and grant us the grace to do what You want us to do. Let us make room in our schedules to honor you. Please help us to be welcoming, helpful, giving, and kind. Our actions are a reflection of our devotion to You. Lord, teach us today the way of love. We pledge to put our hearts, minds, and souls into loving You, our neighbors, and ourselves. In the Sacred and Precious Name of Jesus, Amen.

Reflection

Following God's word leads to a life of righteousness. Which Bible verse do you abide by? What advice would you give those who struggle to live a moral life?

Experiencing the Love of God

*

Let love be without dissimulation. Abhor that which is evil;

cleave to that which is good.

Romans 12:9

Prayer

Lord, make your love known to us. Don't allow the feeling of your love to go away. Provide us with the experience of loving and being loved by you. Grant us the fortitude and determination to know You well through any and all circumstances. Guide us as we grow in our capacity to love and be loved by You and those closest to us. Lord, show us how to love You. May it be an unshakeable love that lasts forever. Amen.

Reflection

As we better understand God, our relationship with him becomes more profound and intimate. What do you think of your relationship with God? What steps do you take to learn more about him?

Seeing The Good In Others

*

See that none render evil for evil unto any man; but ever follow that which is good, both among yourselves, and to all men.

1 Thessalonians 5:15

Prayer

Lord, make us people who actively look for and testify to the goodness in others. You bestowed these beautiful qualities onto us; may we learn to share them with everyone we meet. Lord, give us the serenity and patience to treat these thorny situations and people with grace and a cheerful attitude. We ask that You provide tranquility to their hearts as well. Do something to provide them with that indescribable happiness. Amen.

Reflection

We should always be kind to others, especially those who are challenging to get along with. How do you cope with difficult individuals? Why should we show them more kindness?

Forgiving Difficult Persons In Your Life

"Whenever you stand praying, forgive, if you have anything against anyone; so that your Father in heaven may also forgive you your trespasses"

Mark 11:25

Prayer

Lord, grant us the grace to embrace and forgive everyone, even those who have wronged or treated us poorly. Keep us from sinning against You by taking charge of our minds, bodies, and tongues. In times like these, help us put aside our desire for vengeance to live in harmony with You and the world around us. We ask this in the holiest name of Jesus Christ. Amen.

Reflection

We should always strive to be forgiving, as this reflects God's affection. What does forgiveness mean to you? How do you ask for forgiveness from someone you have wronged?

Prayer to Heal My Broken Heart

Nor height, nor depth, nor any other creature, shall be able to separate us from the love of God, which is in Christ Jesus our Lord.

Romans 8:39

Prayer

God in heaven, please wipe away my tears. Please accept me into Your loving arms and shower me with Your everlasting affection. You mend the hearts of the shattered, Lord. You're putting bandages on my broken heart. Help me through this challenging moment by being my guidance and my comfort. And when night falls, and anxiety rises inside me, may you be the light that fills my soul with happiness. Amen.

✱

Reflection

God restores us to wholeness after we have been wounded through his love. Have you ever been broken before? How did God heal you of your wounds?

Daily Prayer Book for Boys

PART 6

Prayers for Spiritual Growth

Activating The Power Of Your Words

✻

But what saith it? The word is nigh thee, even in thy mouth, and in thy heart: that is, the word of faith, which we preach. That if thou shalt confess with thy mouth the Lord Jesus, and shalt believe in thine heart that God hath raised him from the dead, thou shalt be saved. For with the heart man believeth unto righteousness; and with the mouth confession is made unto salvation.

Romans 10:8-10

Prayer

Dear God in the heavens, I humbly beseech you now to release the force of my words. Give me the wisdom to use my words to deliver blessings rather than curses, life rather than death. Please help me find the right words to say to people suffering so that I might bring them comfort and hope. I want to use my words to bring praise and adoration to your name and be a beacon of hope in this world. May I never forget that my words have the ability to bring about either life or death. Amen.

✳

Reflection

Since words can destroy a person's essence, we should always use kind language when communicating with others. Have you spoken negatively to others? How can words affect a person's self-esteem?

Prayer For Patience

For whatsoever things were written aforetime were written for our learning, that we through patience and comfort of the scriptures might have hope.

Romans 15:4

Prayer

I surrender all to You, Lord since You alone are worthy of all glory, honor, and acclaim. God, please open my eyes. Give me the ability to control my temper and the tolerance to see the good in people. Please show me the many ways in which You have provided for me. Please help me open my heart to You and Your Word daily. Please help me be receptive to Your lessons and open my mind. Amen.

✳

Reflection

When we are furious, we should not control our emotions and be patient with difficult people. How do you maintain self-control? Why do we need patience when interacting with others?

Reliance On God

*

Hast thou not known? Hast thou not heard, that the everlasting God, the Lord, the Creator of the ends of the earth, fainteth not, neither is weary? There is no searching of his understanding. He giveth power to the faint; and to them that have no might he increaseth strength.

Isaiah 40:28-29

Prayer

No one else is as great as You, Lord. Let me apologize for my lack of trust. You, who see within my soul, please rescue me and renew my hope in You. I have my doubts about You a lot, Father. But in You, Oh Lord, I trust and see the whole picture in Your good and perfect time. Amen.

✱

Reflection

We should always believe God is with us and will answer our petitions. What doubts do you have about God? Why do you continue to believe in him despite your doubts?

I Can Always Count On You

*

O give thanks unto the Lord, for he is good: for his mercy endureth forever.

Psalm 107:1

Prayer

I trust in You, my loving Lord. I beg You to help me because nothing is going as I imagined. As I walk with You, please renew my soul. Help me remember that I can rely on You. I need your power; I am feeble. Oh, Lord, there is so much unpredictability in the world. But I know God can be counted on in every sense of the word. You are the unchanging God whose love is everlasting and unending and who is always there. Trusting in You is easy since You've promised never to abandon me. Amen.

✳

Reflection

Trust in God entails a firm conviction that everything will turn out well due to his power. Do you trust your friends? How do you know that you can rely on them?

Give Us The Courage To Live Boldly

*

Thus saith the Lord; cursed be the man that trusteth in man, and maketh flesh his arm, and whose heart departeth from the Lord.

Jeremiah 17:5

Prayer

Lord, Your goodness and kindness are unending. I pray that I may have faith in Your existence. God, my savior, please make me a new person. Make use of me. You will always be the one I turn to for help. Give me the strength I need today to face this terrible world with confidence in You and the resolve to live a life of bravery and integrity. I ask this in the name of Jesus Christ, amen.

✳

Reflection

If we have faith in God, we can overcome all obstacles. What motivates you to get up every day? How do you manage your daily difficulties?

Speak Into My Life

*

*For wisdom is a defense, and money is a defense: but the
excellency of knowledge is, that wisdom giveth life to them
that have it.*

Ecclesiastes 7:12

Prayer

Please, Lord, enlighten my mind so that I might learn more about You and Your Word. As I read the Bible, please grant me insight and understanding. Please open my eyes and ears as I listen to the pastor, preacher, or apostle explain the meaning of Your Holy Book for my life. Please enlighten me about Jesus Christ and His teachings so that I may imitate His example. Amen.

✳

Reflection

Bible provides us with a wealth of useful knowledge. How frequently do you study the Bible? What is the most significant thing you have learned from the Bible?

Bless Me With Divine Knowledge And Wisdom

✳

The fear of the Lord is the beginning of knowledge: but fools despise wisdom and instruction.

Proverbs 1:7

Prayer

Oh, Lord, how I want to spend time in Your Sacred Presence.Please help me to grasp Your lessons when they are given to me. Grant me insight from up high so that I may share my wisdom with the world. In the same way that You were patient, kind, and compassionate when You came to earth to redeem us, please teach me to be those things to my brother. I command and proclaim that the Lord Jesus Christ will open my eyes to new insights and understanding of the Bible. Amen.

❋

Reflection

As stewards of the Lord, it is our duty to impart our acquired knowledge to others. What one piece of wisdom would you like to impart to others? Why would you like to impart this wisdom to others?

Lead Me, Lord, To A Life Of Purity

*

How much more shall the blood of Christ, who through the eternal Spirit offered himself without spot to God, purge your conscience from dead works to serve the living God?

Hebrews 9:14

Prayer

Guide me, Lord, to live a pure life. Please give me the ability to keep this up permanently. Show me the simple road to proper living. When I wander, please guide me back to Your loving arms as my eternal Father. Oh Lord, make me a beacon that draws others out of the shadows so they may see Your glory when they gaze at me. Make me as pure as snow by washing away my sins. Lord, make me new. Have Your way with my tongue, lifestyle, and sins, for I am being made new, not fitting into the pattern of this world. Amen.

❋

Reflection

We should always aspire to purity and avoid engaging in immoral behavior. How frequently do you attend confession? How do you resist the temptation to sin?

Daily Prayer Book for Boys

Encouragement to Continue Praying

"But when ye pray, use not vain repetitions, as the heathen do: for they think that they shall be heard for their much speaking."

- Matthew 6:7

God gave us the ability to pray as one of the greatest blessings when He made us. Incredibly, we can have personal conversations with God no matter when or where we choose. When our faith develops and we get closer to God, praying may seem like a routine we check off like an item on a 'to-do list.' It's easy to let prayer go by the wayside as our schedules become busier, but that doesn't have to be the case.

God has commanded us to pray; therefore, that's a good reason to do it. Prayer must be a regular component of our life in Christ if we are to do what He asks of us. One's obedience is shown via prayer. We must answer God's command to pray. You can accomplish all things with God's help. God can handle whatever you bring to Him, so feel free to tell Him anything. Praying in a new position is refreshing. Praying briefly at various times during the day may help us get closer to God and bring great blessings.

Praise and adoration of God are facilitated through prayer. It's a way for us to admit wrongdoing and be forgiven, which we hope will result in true regret. Moreover, prayer allows us to make our needs known to God. Essentially, all of these forms of prayer include speaking to God. He is interested in a one-on-one relationship with us and wants to hear from us when we pray. Communicating with the eternal God is the primary goal of prayer, yet receiving God's favor is also appropriate. When people stop talking to one another, the connection quickly deteriorates. Likewise, when we stop talking to

God, our connection with Him deteriorates.

Does God need our help? No. He has absolute power and rules over all He has made. That begs the question: why do we have to pray? For the simple reason that God has designated prayer as the channel via which certain things may take place. The love of Jesus may be shared with others via prayer. When people pray, they remove their limitations and allow God to act. It's not that God can't do anything without our praying; prayer is an integral aspect of His strategy for bringing about His will on Earth.

Praying does make a difference. Prayers for one another are a powerful demonstration of God's presence and power among God's people. God hears believers' prayers, and he can do mighty things. Take a risk and pray for the people and situations that seem most in need. By praying for them and bringing their needs before God, you may be their greatest gift.

Daily Prayer Book for Boys

Quiz Questions

Complete the Sentence

1. For God so loved the world, that he gave his only begotten Son, that whosoever believeth in him should not perish, but have _____.

    a. everlasting life

    b. blessed life

    c. holy life

2. And into whatsoever house ye enter, first say, _____ be to this house. And if the son of peace be there, your peace shall rest upon it: if not, it shall turn to you again.

    a. blessed

    b. peace

    c. understanding

3. They that sow in _____ shall reap in joy.

a. sadness

b. sorrow

c. tears

4. For I know the thoughts that I think toward you, saith the Lord, thoughts of peace, and not of _____, to give you an expected end.

a. sin

b. emptation

c. evil

5. O give thanks unto the Lord; for he is good; for his _____ endureth forever.

a. mercy

b. love

c. peace

6. Continue in prayer, and watch in the same with _____.

a. thanksgiving

b. adoration

c. fear

7. Husbands, love your wives, even as Christ also loved the _____, and gave himself for it.

a. heaven

b. church

c. house

8. Let not mercy and truth forsake thee: bind them about thy neck; write them upon the table of thine _____. So shall thou find favor and good understanding in the sight of God and man.

a. mind

b. soul

c. heart

9. But God commendeth his _____ toward us, in that, while we were yet sinners, Christ died for us.

a, love

b. wisdom

c. words

10. Let love be without dissimulation. _____ that which is evil; cleave to that which is good.

a. accept

b. abhor

c. learn

11 For wisdom is a defense, and money is a defense: but the _____ of knowledge is, that wisdom giveth life to them that have it.

a. positivity

b. excellency

c. purity

12. The fear of the Lord is the beginning of _____: but fools despise wisdom and instruction.

a. life

b. love

c. knowledge

Answers:

1. a. everlasting life

2. b. peace

3. c. tears

4. c. evil

5. a. mercy

6. a. thanksgiving

7. b. church

8. c. heart

9. a. love

10. b. abhor

11. b. excellency

12. c. knowledge

Don't Forget Your Free Bonus Downloads!

As our way of saying thank you, we've included in every purchase bonus gift downloads. If you've enjoyed reading this book, please consider leaving a review.

Or Scan Your Phone to open QR code

About Us

FaithLabs is a faith-based publisher dedicated to producing books that inspire and uplift readers.

With a focus on Christian values and principles, FaithLab's team of experienced editors work closely with authors to bring their messages of hope and faith to life. From devotional books to inspirational memoirs, FaithLabs offers a range of titles to deepen readers' spiritual journeys.

Thanks for reading,

FAITH LABS